# 1984

# NOTES

*including*
- *Orwell's Life and Career*
- *1984 and Anti-Utopian Fiction*
- *Brief Synopsis*
- *List of Characters*
- *Chapter Commentaries*
- *Character Analyses*
- *"Is the World of 1984 Possible?"*
- *Alienation in 1984*
- *Love in 1984*
- *Plot, Style, and Structure*
- *Humanity and Society in 1984*
- *Key Quotations in 1984*
- *1984 Game Page and Essay Topics*
- *Selected Bibliography*

*by*
*Gilbert Borman, J.D.*
*Detroit College of Law*

INCORPORATED

LINCOLN, NEBRASKA 68501

**Editor**

Gary Carey, M.A.
University of Colorado

**Consulting Editor**

James L. Roberts, Ph.D.
Department of English
University of Nebraska

ISBN 0-8220-0899-8
© Copyright 1984
by
**Cliffs Notes, Inc.**
All Rights Reserved
Printed in U.S.A.

1998 Printing

Cliffs Notes, Inc.          Lincoln, Nebraska

# CONTENTS

# 1984 NOTES

## ORWELL'S LIFE AND CAREER

George Orwell, whose real name was Eric Blair, was born in 1903, in Bengal, India, the son of a minor official in the Indian Civil Service. As was customary, his mother brought him back to England when he was eight to be educated, along with his two sisters. Orwell was sent to a boarding school on the South Coast, a school whose students were largely sons of the wealthy. To attract such students, the school concentrated mainly on "cramming" boys for entrance to Harrow and Eton. Orwell was one of a few boys allowed to attend at a lower tuition, a practice followed to insure the winning of scholarships for the honor of the school. He came from what he himself called the "lower-upper-middle class" and hence was subjected to the snobbery of the other boys and the headmaster and his wife.

Orwell went to Eton in 1917 on a scholarship. The atmosphere was freer there, he made friends, and he read a good deal. He also encountered, for the first time, popular liberal and socialist ideas. Such ideas were common subjects of discussion at Eton, especially in the period immediately following the First World War. When he graduated in 1921, he decided not to go on to a university, although he could have. Instead, he joined the Civil Service and went to Burma as a sergeant in the Indian Imperial Police.

Orwell served in Burma from 1922 to 1927. As a policeman he was, of course, the embodiment of British imperialism to the natives, a painful reversal of roles in comparison with his life as a schoolboy. He intensely disliked being the instrument by which power was exercised over the Burmese; on the other hand, he had to play the part of one in authority. When he returned to England on leave in 1927, he resigned his post.

For various reasons, not all of them clear even to Orwell himself, he deliberately chose to live among working-class people in Paris and among tramps in England for more than a year. These experiences formed the basis for his first book, an autobiographical work he called *Down and Out in Paris and London*, published in 1933. Although he had published some early writing under his real name, this first book used the name *George Orwell*. He later explained that he took the last name from an English river near which he had once lived and the first name as being typically English. In any case, it was probably a symbolic act signaling his choice of vocation as well as his attitude toward his own country.

During these years Orwell worked as a teacher, and after he married he and his wife kept a village pub and a village general store. His income was small, and his first book brought him very little. His first novel, *Burmese Days*, based on his experiences in Burma, came out in 1934. In 1935 he published another novel, *A Clergyman's Daughter*, which makes use, in part, of his teaching experience.

Although by now he had received critical comment in a few places, Orwell was not making enough income from his writing to depend on it entirely. His novel *Keep the Aspidistra Flying*, published in 1936, was based on his experiences at this time as a clerk in a bookstore. He became a socialist during this period, and when his publisher encouraged him to visit a depressed industrial area and write about his personal reactions, he took the opportunity to put his political convictions into action. The results of this trip, *The Road to Wigan Pier*, came out in 1937.

Meanwhile, the Spanish Civil War had broken out, and although Orwell went as an observer and reporter, he found himself enlisting on the Republican side. By chance, he joined a militia loyal to P.O.U.M., a Marxist, anti-Stalinist political party, rather than the better known (at least in America at the time) International Brigade, which was ultimately Communist-controlled. He was badly wounded on the front, and by the time he recovered from the wound the Republican government was dominated by Communist groups responsive to direction from Russia, and the purge of other political parties, including the P.O.U.M., was under way. Orwell and his wife were forced to leave Spain for fear of imprisonment and possible summary execution. His experiences in the Spanish Civil War are recorded in *Homage to Catalonia*, published in 1938.

Upon his return to England, Orwell published another novel, *Coming Up for Air*, in 1939. This was the first of his books to sell at all well. The war which he had predicted in this book was soon under way, and although he tried to get into the army, he was rejected for service because of his health. In spite of the tuberculosis from which he suffered all his life, he was accepted in the Home Guard. During the Second World War, he worked for a time with the Indian Service of the British Broadcasting Corporation.

Two more books, collections of essays, appeared in 1940 and 1941: *Inside the Whale, and Other Essays* and *The Lion and the Unicorn: Socialism and the English Genius.* In addition, during this time, Orwell did a great deal of political writing. A regular column, "As I Please," appeared in the *London Tribune*; and he contributed to the *Observer, Manchester Evening News, Partisan Review,* and *New Leader.*

In 1945, Orwell published the first of the two books for which he is generally known, *Animal Farm.* Like *1984,* an anti-utopian novel, it is cast in the form of an animal satire. The obvious subject of the satire is Soviet Russia, but more generally it has to do with totalitarianism of any kind. The success of the book, especially in the United States, gave Orwell an income he had never before enjoyed.

*Dickens, Dalí, and Others: Studies in Popular Culture,* another collection of essays, appeared in 1946. With the death of his wife in the same year, Orwell had the complete care of his adopted son.

In order to find the time to complete a book which embodied the ideas that concerned him most at this time, he moved to the Scottish Hebrides. His most celebrated book, *1984,* was published in 1949. In it, Orwell represents a society of the near future which is a projection of certain aspects of life in the contemporary world. Although he remarried and was planning new work for the future, Orwell died in London, in early 1950, from poor health and exhaustion.

Two other collections of essays appeared shortly after his death: *Shooting an Elephant, and Other Essays,* in 1950, and *Such, Such Were the Joys,* in 1953.

## *1984* AND ANTI-UTOPIAN FICTION

The tradition of utopian fiction — fiction predicated on the possibility of a perfect existence for man — is very old, as old as the story of the Garden of Eden in Genesis, at least for the Western world. It embodies both nostalgia for a legendary Golden Age and hope for the way man might live in some distant future.

Although *The Republic* of Plato is older, the name for this kind of fiction comes from Sir Thomas More's *Utopia*, published in Latin in 1516. In it, a character discovers a land called Utopia, or Nowhere Land. A popular work, it was translated into English in 1551, and has since served as a model for writers who share More's purpose. Francis Bacon's *The New Atlantis* (1626) and Jonathan Swift's *Gulliver's Travels* (1726) are further examples of utopian novels.

The nineteenth century was particularly interested in the idea of utopia, both in literature and in social experiments. In English literature there are books like Samuel Butler's *Erewhon* – "nowhere" spelled backward – (1872) and William Morris's *News from Nowhere* (1891). Tennyson, in "Locksley Hall" (1842), writes of seeing a "vision of the world" in which finally man learns to live at peace with himself in a "federation of the world."

In American literature, Edward Bellamy's *Looking Backward* (1888) and Herman Melville's *Typee* (1846) and *Omoo* (1847) are examples of the same impulse to see man in an uncorrupted state. This desire is related to the phenomenon of the frontier in American history. The West allowed the possibility of establishing an ideal society or community free of the historical evils that man had always suffered in Europe. When the peaceful community that Huckleberry Finn and his companion Jim establish on the raft is disrupted by the world, Huck eventually decides to "light out for the Territory." Twain accurately reflects, in *The Adventures of Huckleberry Finn* (1884), the impulse to flee to the frontier and away from civilization. This is echoed in our own time in Holden Caulfield's desire to establish a community of the innocent somwhere in the West, in J. D. Salinger's *The Catcher in the Rye*.

Men in the nineteenth century believed in the perfectability of mankind and in the real possibility of an ultimate utopia, a time when all men would be able to live together in a united world in a state of peace. But the events of history in the twentieth century have undermined that belief. Both cold and hot wars have followed each other in quick succession; revolutions and civil wars have clouded the orderly progress of man toward some better future. Totalitarianism has become a fact that can hardly be ignored, from Hitler's Germany to the Russia of Stalin and later Soviet leaders. The doctrine that man can be directed for purposes other than that of developing the best in his nature is, of course, directly opposed to the belief in man's perfectability.

In our time has arisen what some critics call the anti-utopian novel – that kind of fiction which shows man at the mercy of a purpose over which he has no control. Not man perfected but man perverted – this is the way the anti-utopian novel views the future. The motive for this new kind of novel may arise from the certainty that man can now destroy not only himself as an individual but all of mankind, that governments can bend people to any kind of purpose whatsoever. Usually such anti-utopian novels are intended as a criticism of the time in which the author lives, much as was the case with nineteenth-century utopian novels.

Shortly after *Animal Farm*, itself an anti-utopian novel, Orwell published a brief essay on the Russian writer Eugene Zamiatin's *We*, which, although it appeared in 1924, was little known to English-speaking readers. It is said by some critics that there are similarities between *1984* and *We*. Certainly Orwell was much impressed by the novel, and he read it during the time when he was thinking about his own *1984*. In his essay on *We*, Orwell himself says that it bears some resemblances to Aldous Huxley's *Brave New World* (1932), but in his opinion is a better novel.

That three writers in the same time, all interested in the idea of anti-utopia, should produce books with some similarities is hardly a surprise. Of the three, only Orwell's depicts a society whose purpose is solely that of power. For this reason, *1984* has caused more discussion and has made more readers uneasy than either of the other two, although Zamiatin's novel is still not well known to the Western world.

The anti-utopian novel is a specialized branch of fiction, like the novel of ideas, for instance. And it is true that the author of such a novel is mainly concerned with depicting a certain kind of society. But since he is writing a novel, by necessity he must use the means available to any novelist: plot, setting, characterization, point of view, structure, and the like. To say that he bends these formal aspects to his purpose is only to describe what any good novelist does. The success with which he makes the reader accept the reality he has created is the only meaningful test of his ability as a writer. Orwell, after all, had written several novels before he produced either *Animal Farm* or *1984*. By the time of these later books he was no longer satisfied with the novel as he had written it and turned to the anti-utopian novel as the most effective means to embody his urgent purposes.

# BRIEF SYNOPSIS

Winston Smith, who works in the Records Department of the Ministry of Truth, revising the past as it appears in newspapers, is dissatisfied living under the inflexible, outwardly paternalistic government of Oceania, epitomized in the ever-present picture of Big Brother. His dissatisfaction increased by the austerity characteristic of daily life, at first he rebels in small ways: writing in a diary, an act viewed with suspicion by the Thought Police; speculating about the political orthodoxy of O'Brien, an important official in the governing oligarchy; becoming unaccountably disturbed by a young woman who watches him; dreaming, over and over, of an idyllic scene in which sexual expression is as natural as the landscape. Winston even goes among the proles, the excluded class, seeking some kind, any kind. of human contact. The young woman, Julia, instigates a liaison between herself and Winston, and they make love in a scene exactly like that in his dream. He knows that their lovemaking is political in meaning; it is his overt act of rebellion against Oceania.

Winston and Julia, their relationship becoming domestic, rent a room to which they can go to be apart from others. Winston and O'Brien meet, the latter taking the initiative, and Winston and Julia together visit O'Brien in his quarters. He leads them to believe he is also in revolt and allows Winston to read a seditious book. Just when Winston is certain that he and Julia will soon be detected – from the beginning he has had little hope they will not be – they are arrested in their rented room.

Winston and Julia are imprisoned separately in the Ministry of Love, and Winston is given over to O'Brien for what he learns will be his complete "rehabilitation," not immediate execution. By physical and then psychological torture, O'Brien puts Winston through the first two stages of his retraining: learning what is expected of him; then understanding it. During the process, Winston comes almost to love O'Brien; together day after day for nine months, they converse finally as if friends.

Preparation for the final stage in Winston's education, acceptance, comes in the dreaded Room 101, where Winston is made to face what he secretly fears most. Completely subjugated – physically, emotionally, and mentally – Winston is released. Upon the occasion of a threatened attack on Oceania and the defeat of the enemy, Winston feels gratitude for, and love for, Big Brother.

# LIST OF CHARACTERS

**Winston Smith**

A physically insignificant man of thirty-nine and a member of the Outer Party who, though not extraordinary in either intelligence or character, rebels against the impersonality and inhumanity of life in the society of Oceania.

**Julia**

A sensually attractive young woman of twenty-six who willingly forms a liaison with Winston, in his act of rebellion, out of a desire on her part solely for companionship and sexual gratification.

**O'Brien**

A vigorous, shrewd, intelligent man of mysteriously high rank in the Inner Party who as Winston's torturer, father confessor, schoolmaster, and even apparent friend, at the last, represents the oligarchy governing Oceania.

**Parsons**

A fellow worker in the Ministry of Truth who acts like a middle-aged Boy Scout and who is proud of his two small children active in the Spies.

**Tillotson**

A man who works across the hall from Winston, in the Records Department.

**Syme**

A philologist working on the eleventh edition of the Newspeak Dictionary, in the Research Department of the Ministry of Truth.

**Mr. Charrington**

Proprietor of a secondhand shop who rents the room on the second floor to Winston and Julia and who turns out to be a member of the Thought Police.

**Ampleforth**

A poet who works in the Ministry of Truth.

# CHAPTER COMMENTARIES

## PART ONE

### CHAPTERS 1-2

The society of Oceania is presented in the first chapter so that the reader is ready to accept it as plausible, not so much by a suspension of disbelief, but rather by an extension of belief. Oceania is not far distant from the reality of the Soviet Union or Nazi Germany, or even wartime England. The physical scene is familiar and only slightly distorted. The devices of the Thought Police are not impossible; in fact, in terms of contemporary technology, they are a little out of date.

An interesting question arises over the name *O'Brien*. Orwell is a careful and thoughtful writer and would not choose a name carelessly. All writers choose names to support characterization or to lend some significance to plot. O'Brien is obviously an Irish name. The man is a member of the Inner Party, and he bears some physical resemblance to Big Brother himself. In a society like that of England, the Irish hold a unique place. They are, to a certain extent, a classless people in a society which is traditionally stratified.

It is possible that O'Brien represents the ideal of the kind of totalitarian state imagined by Orwell—a truly classless individual who has achieved membership in the Inner Party by the very reason of his exclusion from the caste system of the old order. He has no first name because, as an important member of the Inner Party, he doesn't need one. He is shown later to live a life of relative luxury, which is in contrast to his outward appearance and in even more striking contrast to his occupation. He is the one who expounds to Winston the doctrines of the Party; he understands them so well because he helped to create them.

At this point in the novel, the girl is nameless. It is not until the act of "thoughtcrime" has been consummated that her name is revealed. It is also insignificant that Winston assumes her to be a member of the Thought Police, while he considers O'Brien to be a conspirator. His ideas are exactly the reverse of reality. Here is one of the main points of the novel: that any sane man, by standards commonly accepted in societies more liberal than Oceania, really stands diametrically opposed to the thinking of "Ingsoc," that his views are the complete reverse of the reality of such a society. Frequently during the course of the novel, and especially in the last section, Winston sees his position as the reverse of the Party's. The process of bringing Winston into accord with the thinking of the Party results in the destruction of the man.

Orwell seems to believe that a society can be controlled through its children. In this section, as in many of the early chapters, there is a suggestion of the inevitable destruction of given individuals. Here, Winston recognizes the fact that these children will ultimately betray their parents to the Thought Police. The children are one more link in the Party's control over the private life of every citizen.

Winston demonstrates a curious dualism in his thinking: he recognizes that he is guilty of thoughtcrime and that the result of thoughtcrime is death, but at the same time he assumes that he is so far undetected. Being undetected, he very much wants to remain alive and to escape detection. As later events will reveal, he is quite wrong in his assumptions. The reader knows, and Winston knows, that he will be caught, but both Winston and the reader have faith that the inevitable can be avoided. Were this not true, Winston could not have committed his thoughtcrime, and the reader would not go on reading the book; and that in itself is an example of "doublethink."

## CHAPTERS 3-5

Winston is depressed by the terrible impersonality of the society he lives in. He doesn't even know some of his co-workers by name. A certain amount of impersonality is common to all metropolitan areas, but that of Winston's world is different. It is an impersonality based on fear, the fear that anyone encountered may be a member of the Thought Police and may betray you.

The people around Winston are, as he is, common and unattractive. The interesting thing, of course, is the startling resemblance between the social and political ideals proposed by the Party and the figures that appear in the advertising that we are all exposed to every day. The people in the advertisements are young, beautiful, desirable, and comfortable, as most of the observers of advertising are not.

Orwell was much concerned about the very close relationship between advertising and propaganda. In many languages there are not two words, as there are in English, to distinguish between these two functions. They are considered synonymous. By showing how important the telescreen and its images are in the society of Oceania, Orwell also shows how important advertising and its ideals have become in our own society. The methods of advertising work as well for political ideologies as they do for refrigerators and washing machines.

The lecture delivered by Syme on the nature of Newspeak is an important part of this section. Newspeak is one of the devices the Party uses to control its members. When Newspeak is perfected, thoughtcrime will be impossible. Syme's conclusion, "Orthodoxy is unconsciousness," is most interesting, since it precludes the existence of any but rote intelligence within the Party. The conscious intelligence cannot be orthodox and therefore is subject to inevitable "vaporization."

The point of Winston's reverie involves "the mutability of the past." This whole question forms one of the bases of the entire plot. The Party is in the act of abolishing the past: it carefully alters facts to suit its current situation. That is Winston's task at the Ministry of Truth: to alter the past to suit the present. Winston's memory retains facts and fragments of facts which do not agree with the present facts of the Party; for example, he remembers that in the past the enemy has changed a number of times, but the Party at the moment maintains that Eurasia has always been the enemy. He is also, in the course of his work, required to revise a promise about the chocolate ration. Winston is terrified of the fact that the Party can literally decide that an event has not occurred and the very act of saying it removes the event from history.

The same is true of individuals. Persons who have been purged by the Party, if they are referred to at all, are known as "unpersons," because they do not exist and never have. All reference to them is purged along with them. No appeal to posterity is possible. Winston's diary will not survive him, and he will cease to exist, like any other unperson. To Winston, this is far worse than torture and death.

The instructor in physical education is intended to be reminiscent of Soviet women. She is the useful female of totalitarian cultures. She will form an instructive contrast to the girl later in the novel. More significantly, she and her exercises epitomize the regimentation of the society.

## CHAPTERS 6-8

The Party's concept of history strikes the modern reader as absurd. It is a mixture of fact and fancy, disregarding any organizing concept of time; thus, the concepts of capitalism are mixed with concepts of medieval feudalism in a kind of historical montage, but the elements of the montage are disparate and unrelated to what might today be considered reality. The lords' privilege of deflowering virgins, for instance, is attributed to capitalists of the early twentieth century by the historians of Oceania. While the concepts appear slightly insane to modern readers, they are not very distantly removed from the idea of history propounded in the Soviet Union in the late 1920s.

Winston's faith in the "proles" (proletarians), in their ability to revolt, reveals more about him than about the reality of Oceania. There is no indication that the masses ever revolt of themselves. Leadership is usually required. In Oceania, in which any potential leadership is immediately rooted out by the Thought Police and any divergence from orthodox behavior is not tolerated, that leadership is not likely to develop. O'Brien will have a number of interesting things to say about this possibility when he instructs Winston in Party doctrine. Granted the possibility of the world Orwell depicts, of course O'Brien is right and Winston is wrong.

Winston is frustrated in sexual matters as he is in everything else. Ultimately, of course, it is this sexual frustration that leads him to the final thoughtcrime and to his own final destruction. The therapy of confessing in his diary his last sexual experience does not work for Winston. He still longs for the kind of sexual experience which is no longer possible in the society in which he lives. Even his marriage was a complete failure because his wife was trained in a hopeless and mindless frigidity by the Party.

Winston does not, however, understand the purposes of the Party in its advocacy of celibacy and in its attempts to destroy all joy in the sexual act. Much later, when O'Brien instructs Winston in the meaning of the Party's ideas, Winston learns why it is necessary for the Party to snuff out all interest in the sexual act.

Winston believes that the sexual relationship accompanying love will result in a loyalty between individuals that is contrary to the desires of the Party. It is ironic that Winston does achieve such a relationship, even establishes the loyalty that he hoped would grow out of it, but the Party destroys that loyalty. It is the destruction of that loyalty that is part of the retraining process Winston undergoes after his arrest by the Thought Police.

Winston is civilized in the contemporary sense of the word. He is, by the standards of the readers' world, a normal individual, sane enough. By the standards of Oceania, however, he is not sane. He has ideas and beliefs which are not appropriate to that time and place. That is why he must be retrained, indeed why he is guilty of thoughtcrime. Orwell suggests, of course, that in this as in other matters Winston is representative of all men in the Western world. The ideological basis for such a state as Winston lives in already exists; the mechanical means for subjugating the people of such a society already exist. Only the abnegation of freedom is necessary.

Winston has made a serious attempt to establish contact with the past. He is drawn to the past to determine whether or not history is mutable, to find the truth. These are all very serious crimes in Oceania. Curiosity is a thoughtcrime, and Winston is a thought-criminal. He is ready now, by the confluence of circumstances, to commit the ultimate thoughtcrime.

The first part of the novel comprises about one-third of the text. It sets the physical scene, the London of Oceania in 1984. It establishes the characters: the central figure is Winston Smith, a minority of one in a totalitarian state. And it sets the political scene, a state in which absolute control is exercised over the life of every individual by regulation of privacy, destruction of language, and the elimination of eroticism. The first part sets the scene for Winston's final crime by bringing into play a series of forces which prepare him for the commission of the crime, which, in fact, make the crime inevitable. The next part will deal with the inevitable outgrowth of the first, as the last part will deal with the inevitable outgrowth of the second.

# PART TWO

## CHAPTERS 1-2

Winston's readiness to enter into a liaison, to accept Julia's advances at face value rather than to question them as a possible trap, indicates that he is ready for thoughtcrime. His dissatisfaction with life and his sexual frustration make him ripe for the occasion.

But in terms of the inevitable conclusion of events, this section may be considered the beginning of the end. By allowing himself to be drawn into the adventure, Winston is condemning himself. Although at the close of Part One he is ripe for thoughtcrime, he might still have drawn back; but when he accepts the girl's advances, he is completely doomed. At the moment when he reads the note, it becomes important for him to remain alive, not to take unnecessary risks. But at the same instant, the risk no longer matters. This is another instance of Winston's duality of mind. This state of mind will characterize him throughout the entire second part. Or to put it still another way, Winston has learned to hope, but he has learned to hope at the very moment when he has placed himself in a hopeless situation. In this situation, it is important to notice that the girl herself is only a means.

The irony of the lovemaking between Winston and Julia is important. At this point, so close to the event, Winston is not aware of this irony. He will realize it much later. But the reader should recognize its significance. The irony stems from Winston's need to live and his involvement in life occurring exactly at the moment when his time is short because of the very nature of the act itself. The paradox of life and death, of seeing and not seeing, of madness and sanity is at the core of the book. The society which Orwell has created is in itself a paradox. It may or may not exist.

Everything before the idyllic scene in the woods leads up to it, and everything that follows stems from it. In short, this may be considered one of the climaxes of the book. The main climax, however, comes at the end of Part Two, and there is a third climax in the last part. If the movement of the book is conceived of as a series of three overlapping sine curves, this scene marks the apex of the first sine curve. These three sine curves may also be said to represent the three major themes of the book. The first of these themes is physical (erotic) love. The second theme is physical pain rather than love, and the last is psychological destruction or change.

## CHAPTERS 3-4

It has been about two months since Winston and Julia first met. In less than a year, Winston's whole history will be over. Both characters, while conscious that they are bringing the end nearer, are unaware of what the future holds. They expect to be arrested, to be tortured, to be killed; but they do not expect the full horror of reality. They are, for the moment, living in a false paradise.

On the one hand, Julia is completely adapted to escape detection in the complex society in which she lives, but on the other, she is almost an earth goddess committed to the animal-physical joy of living. It is another irony that such a woman should be the immediate cause of death and destruction. She demonstrates to Winston with the warmth of her own body her unthinking conviction that they are far from dead. She has hope. And she tries to teach Winston to hope or at least to believe in some kind of possible future.

But Julia lives from day to day, from sexual encounter to sexual encounter. She is not concerned with the kinds of ideas that trouble Winston. She is concerned with the immediate causes of living, not with the abstract causes of dying. She would have committed the act of murder which Winston in his more thoughtful way was unable to commit. Her view of the world, of course, is just as unrealistic and just as dualistic as Winston's, but from quite a different starting point.

Winston, under the influence of Julia, is slowly drifting toward a more physical orientation. Having lived in celibacy for nearly a dozen years and having had virtually no sex life during his marriage, he is emotionally immature. His immaturity displays itself in this situation, as the emotional immaturity of an adolescent displays itself in an initial romance. Winston is a case of arrested development. Now that he has been freed to develop, his view of the world will become more unrealistic. Already he is extending the possible time of his relationship. In actuality, of course, they have very little time.

Several symbols of importance appear in this section. The most striking, immediately, is the glass paperweight; for Winston it becomes a miniature world in which he can see himself and Julia safe from change and from life under Big Brother. The print of St. Clement's and the jingle about London churches remind him of the past, which is important both to him and to the Party. Winston's fear of rats, dropped in here so unobtrusively, seems unimportant at the moment. In fact, the meaning of all these symbols will change greatly in later incidents.

## CHAPTERS 5-8

Julia's understanding of the ways in which Party ideas work is much keener than Winston's, although she accepts unthinkingly much of its mythology. She believes that the Party invented airplanes and that Oceania has always been at war with Eurasia. The whole business of abstract truth does not concern her. Winston tells her about the incident when he held the scrap of evidence in his hand, but Julia does not understand the episode. In short, Winston and Julia fall into a pattern of stereotypical domesticity: the husband makes all the important decisions, about national policy, religious doctrine, space exploration, and the like, while the wife makes all the lesser decisions, about where the next vacation will be spent, how the family money will be used, and so on. Julia is practical, while Winston is something of an idealist and a dreamer.

Orwell's intention is obvious. He wants these two rebels to appear to be very ordinary people. And they are. They are essentially middle-class people with ordinary middle-class desires and needs. They do not really wish to change the world in any radical way; they just want to be left alone to live out their own lives peacefully and quietly. One of the horrors of Oceania is that fulfillment of their wish is quite out of the question.

As the liaison between Winston and Julia becomes increasing like the relationship between husband and wife, first Winston and then both of them engage in the potentially deadly game of seeing O'Brien as a fellow conspirator. Winston is ready for the unexpected meeting with O'Brien and the visit to his quarters, as two months earlier he was willing to accept Julia's instigation of their relationship. Although in the state of mind to rebel, Winston holds back until an occasion makes it possible for him to act.

Winston's belief that no matter what happens to him he can resist in his inner self is perhaps the greatest irony in the book, since the last part is a detailed treatise on exactly how the Party infests itself inside an individual, how his betrayal of himself can be effected, and how he is able not only to rationalize the fact that he has given himself away but come to love the person who has caused him to betray himself.

In this section Winston resolves his guilt feelings about his youth and about his relationship with his mother. But more important, he raises the question of resisting the Party by keeping untouched his innermost self. This belief creates a tension that makes it easy to anticipate the sort of punishment he will face for unorthodox behavior.

### CHAPTERS 9-10

*The Book*, which Winston finally is able to read, is Orwell's parody of Leon Trotsky's *The Revolution Betrayed*. Purportedly written by Emmanuel Goldstein, Oceania's official scapegoat – although Winston learns later that O'Brien himself is responsible for it – it is a means by which Oceania can be revealed, as it were, from both the outside and the inside. It is also used, of course, as additional evidence of Winston's need for retraining.

He reads only parts of two chapters. In these, the rise of Oceania and its relationships to Eurasia and Eastasia are described. More important to Winston, perhaps, is the explanation of the means by which the Inner Party keeps power and the way it creates reality. Ingsoc, the Party's official and expedient ideology, is based on a kind of idealism or, as O'Brien readily admits to Winston later, solipsism. Reality is what the Party deems it to be; and with power over recorded history, that reality can be, and is, altered day by day. It is largely by this means that the Party controls the minds of its citizens.

Having read some of *The Book*, Winston understands only the Party's means, not its ends. The answer to this mystery comes from O'Brien in the Ministry of Love, in Part Three.

The scene of the arrest of Winston and Julia is rather melodramatic. A scene of domesticity is suddenly transformed into an arena of brutality. Winston acts like a man who has all along expected just this scene, perhaps rehearsed it in his dreams. He is more a product of Oceania than he is ever able to realize.

With the arrest of Winston and Julia, the thought and the act — the thoughtcrime — have come to the only conclusion possible in such a closed political system. The consequences are all that remain, the punishment, although Winston is to learn to his surprise that it is not immediate death. Julia will virtually disappear from the story; the last act is to be played out between Winston and O'Brien.

In the scene of the arrest, the symbols mentioned earlier figure prominently. The glass paperweight is smashed by the Thought Police. Behind the print of St. Clement's is a telescreen. The jingle about the bells of the London churches becomes ominous, especially the last line, when repeated by Mr. Charrington. The paperweight especially is reminiscent of an earlier symbol, the "Golden Country," about which Winston dreamed before meeting Julia and seeing his dream become reality. The world which he imagined as existing in the paperweight has vanished now as surely as the world of his dream.

# PART THREE

## CHAPTERS 1-2

Thus, the inevitable, known not only by Winston but by the reader as well from the very first moments of the story, has come about. Winston is in the hands of the Thought Police, and pain, suffering, and confession are no longer inevitable but at hand. The brutality of the prison is made vivid, as well as its sadistic efficiency. These chapters demonstrate brainwashing techniques refined to the ultimate through the use of science in a society gone mad, at least from the point of view of Winston and the reader.

Although O'Brien is the torturer, Winston regards him as his friend. He thinks of the pain as an outside thing and the relief from pain as coming from O'Brien. In Winston's mind the two men are intimates; they can talk together because O'Brien can understand Winston. Winston believes that O'Brien's mind includes his, that O'Brien has already thought every thought he is capable of conceiving. Although O'Brien tortures him and eventually will order his death, Winston senses the same similarity of mind and temperament O'Brien himself comments on.

That a victim should come to love his torturer is part of the process of conversion. It is also – O'Brien points this out to Winston – a refinement on brainwashing techniques as practiced in contemporary totalitarian societies. The conversion must be so total that the victim will thank his tormentors for having converted him and beg to be killed while he is still in a state of grace. And the victim must regard his own death as a benefit, not to himself because it brings a cessation of pain, but to the Party because it is the destruction of an unworthy individual. The erring citizen – Winston – must be reborn, only to be destroyed; Orwell constructs here a cruel parody of Christian resurrection.

## CHAPTERS 3-5

What Winston was unable to discover in *The Book* is now revealed by O'Brien: the Party seeks and holds power for its own sake, not for the way it can be used. And power means the power to make men suffer. This idea of power is an extension of prevalent notions in contemporary societies. We think of power as acquired usually for some end other than itself.

The Party, as expressed in O'Brien's comments to Winston, also believes in a simplified idealism. What it desires to be true, what it is expedient to believe as true, is true. O'Brien presents this idea of reality in such a way that Winston finds it hard to believe, except that O'Brien is in the position to force him to by means of torture.

This view of reality is closely connected with the idea of the alternate past and the control of historical records.

An instance of the Party's creating of reality is the simple addition problem which Winston earlier made into a symbol of freedom and which O'Brien turns into a symbol of rehabilitation. Later, Winston attempts to train himself in the process of doublethink. Though he has been unable to preserve his mind from change by the Party, he believes, even as he tries to master doublethink, that he can keep his heart and spirit free.

Room 101 changes that. The rats that O'Brien uses to move Winston past learning and understanding toward acceptance and love symbolize all that he fears most. Earlier in the novel, with Julia in the room above Mr. Charrington's shop, Winston had been horrified by rats. He betrays Julia; he literally loses his mind. It is almost the last stage in the process in which O'Brien has participated as instructor many times before. All that remains is for Winston to love Big Brother.

## CHAPTER 6

The final, and inevitable, change takes place at this moment; Winston is healed. He demonstrates his sanity by expressing his love of Big Brother.

Thus, in a period covering approximately one calendar year, Winston has gone through the entire cycle. Just about a year earlier, he had his initial contact with Julia. They spent about four months together, and then he was in the Ministry of Love for about nine months, like a child in the womb.

## APPENDIX

The language which Orwell devised as the official language of Oceania – Newspeak – is an extension of what he saw happening in the use of English in his own time: lying and deceit for political purposes. Orwell believed that careless use of language corrupted thought and that inexact thinking had a bad effect on language. For his society of the future, he conceived of a language whose purpose was wholly political, not communicative. Newspeak is another, and powerful, means by which the Party retains its hold over its citizens by making unorthodox thoughts impossible. If there are no words for unacceptable ideas of thoughts, they will cease to exist or to be a threat to those in power. He projects this use of language to its ultimate end: the complete silencing of speech and therefore thought. The ideal response for the sake of orthodoxy is inarticulate noise, or "duckspeak."

Orwell's creation of the new language is ingenious; for instance, he uses the present characteristic of the language called functional shift (the tendency of words to move easily from one part of speech to another). He also gives examples of the use of Newspeak during the course of the story. One example which reveals especially well what Newspeak is like is the order to Winston in Newspeak – which is translated into "Oldspeak" or Standard English – to revise a speech of Big Brother's.

## CHARACTER ANALYSES

### Winston Smith

Smith is Orwell's chief protagonist; as readers, we rely on him to be our camera and our interpreter of a bizarre world. He is designed to touch our deepest sentiments, embody most of the central concepts of the novel, and ultimately force us to accept ideas that are sometimes uncomfortable to accept. Even his name is part of the masterful design which Orwell uses to mold the world of *1984*. His first name is that of perhaps the greatest statesman of the century: Winston Churchill. His surname is that of the most common name in our language: Smith. Thus, Winston's name contains one of the many paradoxes presented in the novel – that is, he is common *and* he is uncommon. His position as a member of the Party should make him exalted, but, in fact, he has the least freedom of all. Orwell does not do this out of coincidence; he deliberately establishes the drastic differences in ideas and ideals between life in Oceania and life in postwar England. Winston is meant to be very much like us; we instinctively like him. He represents our own feelings and experiences, he responds, feels and acts as we should, and his destruction is something painful to behold because his destruction *could* be our own destruction. We often like to view ourselves as ordinary people with ordinary ideas, leading ordinary lives. Our self-identity with Winston creates great empathy between the reader and Winston; therefore, his savage debasement seems outrageous. Orwell manipulates Winston to achieve the greatest impact possible on us.

Winston is clearly a tragic figure because his failure is total, and his suffering almost beyond imagination. We are attracted to his innocence, and we are repelled by the cruelty of his fate. His basic conclusions about reality and the Party are right, but in so many things he is wrong and his naiveté results in even more suffering. He often understands *how*, but he can't imagine *why*. Ultimately, we learn that how and why are not important. The essence of Ingsoc, control of thought and action, must be resisted completely at its inception or, we realize, we might well end up like Winston, and he is unable to do anything more than dream that, hopefully, *someone else* will stop the Party. Winston is our underdog, and we cheer on his hopeless cause.

Our first meeting with Winston sets the tone for all of our later dealings with him. We see the ugliness of his world, and we also see the degradation of his existence. He drinks, his body is ravaged by neglect, and we realize that he is powerless to improve the conditions of his life. He is lonely, broke, and suicidal. He cannot afford a pair of pajamas, and it is likely that he will never be able to find any. With just a few words, Orwell makes us feel compelled to share Winston's pain and misery; we share his secret hope that things *will* get better.

When Winston meets Julia and falls in love with her, things do get better, and for a few moments he is happy. He conspires to join the Brotherhood, and we almost feel that some miracle can happen and that the nightmare can end. Winston's health improves, and the reader enjoys Winston's romantic relationship with Julia; it is heartwarming and compelling. These two people are refugees and heroes, opposing all that we characterize as evil; they are two lovers who must meet in secret in a disapproving world. Their dream is shattered, however, and Winston becomes our witness to the innate evil of man and the mindless brutality that we are capable of inflicting upon one another. When we leave Winston, it is with a numbed shock that this tragedy could happen to anyone – most especially, to us. The indignity that has been heaped on Winston seems almost too much to bear for the reader and Winston. He has been forced to love the very people who did this to him. Being privy to Winston's private thoughts and experiences, we feel close to him. The Thought Police's invasion of Winston's privacy seems like an invasion of our own thoughts and privacy. We feel each punch, each shock, and each fear. Winston is destroyed before our very eyes, and we are as helpless as he is to stop it. He hopes against hope – until we read the novel's four ugly last words: "He loved Big Brother."

At our very deepest emotional and mental centers, we resolve to do what Winston could not do: we will *not* love Big Brother. Winston, while no more real than Big Brother, is a friend of ours, created by Orwell, and we resolve to help our friend and prevent his fate from being ours. This reaction is obviously encouraged by Orwell. Winston embodies many concepts of democracy, freedom, peace, love, and decency; these virtuous ideas are supposedly close to our own. Oceania's violent attack upon them gives us the strength to uphold these ideals. It is the greatest tribute to Orwell's skill as a writer that Winston is so evocative a character and so successful at representing his author's views and getting the reader to respond to them the way he intends.

## Julia

Julia is a far more subtle character than she appears to be. Superficially, she seems to be little more than an object to Winston's sexual desires. This is not borne out, however, on closer examination. Julia embodies forms of revolution that are inconceivable to Winston. She is often more right about the nature of the Party than he is, and she has many abilities that enable her to survive better than Winston. She is far more realistic about the aims of the Party in that she is entirely apathetic to the Party's political thought.

Julia attacks the Party through her own means. Seemingly going through the motions of being a good Party member, she can conceal her cynical apathy towards Party politics and thought. She is entirely disinterested in being able to prove that the Party lies or whether or not Big Brother exists. Even though she has no recollection of any time that the Party has not been in control, she rejects everything that she hears, and thus she is as close to the ultimate truth as Winston or anyone else. In her own way, Julia is doing her best to fight against the Party's ideals and actions. She realizes that a man would have to fear rejection and betrayal if he initiated a sexual advance; thus it falls upon women to get things started (Julia does just this for Winston). A man wouldn't dare make an advance without being sure of the woman's intentions; she could denounce him or be a member of the Thought Police; the consequences of a man's doing something wrong are too grave. Yet, in the repressive atmosphere of Oceania, women (who, like Julia, are untrained in anything other than the Party's sexual code) still revolt – out of common sense of such natural human instincts as love and the desire for companionship. Thus, women can dare to thwart the Party's control.

Julia, for instance, after being careful for a very long time, and out of love for Winston, decides to throw caution to the wind and take the room above Charrington's shop. Unfortunately, she underestimates the ruthlessness and thoroughness of the Thought Police's persecution, and she falls into their net. She stops caring about herself out of selflessness and pays a very heavy price. Ironically, had she continued to live cautiously, she would have fared no better, for the Thought Police were already aware of her "crimes" and knew that they could punish her whenever they wished to.

Julia's sexuality is an irrational weapon against the Party's dogma of chastity and loneliness. But it is a weapon. And there is an even more powerful weapon: love. Love is presented as the only force equal to the Party's hate. The Party's greatest enemy is eroticism, and since passion is love in its most powerful form, Julia's small liaisons are deadly poison indeed. It is interesting to note that the love song manufactured by the Party is more powerful and enduring than the hate song. The old woman who sang in the courtyard preserved the song of love; Orwell thus suggests that the force of love is more powerful than hatred. Until the Party is able to completely control such behavior, women like Julia will continue to appear and eat away at the Party's power. It is in this sense that women present a greater threat to the Party than men do. It should be remembered that at the beginning of the novel, Winston expresses his nearly pathological hatred for women – especially for women who (like his wife and Julia) ostensibly follow the party line. Part of Winston's hate, however, is his jealousy of women's monopoly on sexuality. The Party's war on love has clearly been very successful on Winston.

Julia, like Winston, contains certain paradoxes which offset and complement the ideas that Winston embraces. For example, she is not intellectual, but she is just as capable as a man when opposing the Party's objectives. But, conversely, just as Winston fails to completely understand the Party, Julia also fails to perceive the danger that the Party's intellectual repression and historical rewriting represent to a normal world. Her tacit acceptance of Party history is a victory in and of itself to the Party. Both Julia and Winston are mentally defeated before they have ever begun to fight. By not understanding the nature of the Party, Julia and Winston – as a force against the Party – are reduced in effectiveness without each other, and in different ways, the realization of their inadequacy gives them a further sense of the futility of their resistance. But while Winston is physically deteriorating, Julia is in her prime and is excessively healthy. Yet she is also the victim of Winston's mental aggressions. This aggression is evidence of how far the institution of love has been eradicated in *1984*. Winston envisions smashing her head in with a paving stone, as well as a whole series of other sadomasochistic assaults, ending in her imagined death. When he finally falls in love with Julia, Winston's violent thoughts focus against anyone who would try and separate the two lovers. His anger in the cafeteria is more "normal" by our standards, but it is still little better than childish jealousy.

By contemporary standards, Julia can be viewed as a kind of patronizing characterization of women, and there are many who catagorize her and the role which she plays as being sexist. In the context of Orwell's other writings, this assessment seems fair; in the context of *1984*, however, the labeling is not so easy. The essential role of Julia's rebellion, coupled with her subtle interrelation with the novel's central ideas, makes it difficult to dismiss Julia as simply a radical sexist. She suffers every bit as much as Winston and is subjected to everything that he is – plus more. One can assume that, given the Party's brutality, she suffers one kind of savagery that Winston does not – namely, rape. Thus, the destruction of Julia's personality is every bit as complete as Winston's. And because Julia is younger than Winston, she will have to endure many more years before she gets the long awaited bullet in the back of the head.

## O'Brien

O'Brien is a figure of mystery to the reader. Until the third part of the novel, we think of him as Winston's friend and co-conspirator. Winston thinks that O'Brien is a friend, but there is always an ominous dream: "We shall meet in the place where there is no darkness." All Winston has to go on is one or two knowing looks from O'Brien. O'Brien brings together all of the confusion and paradox of *1984*. As a member of the Inner Party, he is privy to "the truth." Not only is he aware of the Party's lies, but he has helped perpetrate them as well.

At times, Winston sees him as a god or a benefactor, even though his face is brutal and powerful. In the end, we see him as a sadistic monster who totally destroys Winston as a human being by reducing him into something less than life, but little more than death.

O'Brien is just as badly deluded as Winston is. The fact that he is among the few to know the truth does nothing to make him change his loyalties. Indeed, just as he helped write in Goldstein's book that the members of the Inner Party are more deluded than the rest of society, he chooses not to believe that he is more deluded or that the book exists. In his vicious maniacal harangue prior to sending Winston to Room 101, O'Brien declares that the laws of nature can be suspended and altered at will by the Party: "I can float off this floor like a soap bubble, if I wish to." He has come to believe his own lies. It is difficult for the reader to accept the proposition that O'Brien really does want to help Winston and is sincere in his promise to make him "perfect." But, by using doublethink, anything at all can be justified or believed. O'Brien can hold two contradictory thoughts in his mind and let them simultaneously exist together and not view them as anything other than a part of a single truth. O'Brien has become Doublethink.

At first, O'Brien's cruelty seems almost *too* enormous. It is not, however, and it is unfortunate that our recent history has shown that people like O'Brien do exist and are capable of, literally, anything. Hitler and Stalin could obliterate tens of millions of innocent lives and, all the while, believe that they were saviors of mankind. Such world leaders care little about the cost to others; they are content to pursue power as an end in itself. Tragically, they continue finding real, or imagined, enemies to slaughter and continue to brutalize them until they themselves are either stopped, purged, or killed.

How is it possible that some people see O'Brien as Winston's friend? How can he help Winston by "making him perfect"? O'Brien's help, in our view, is an abominable sin against everything which we believe and hold dear in our society. But, in the Party's point of view, O'Brien is doing the right thing. Doublethink has worked in the past and will work in the future. In contemporary history, the Soviet Union has been accused of using psychiatric hospitals and mind-bending, hallucinogenic drugs to destroy political dissenters. The Nazis conducted barbaric experiments on living people to discover supposed differences between other peoples and the Nazis' concept of a Master

Race. Even soldiers fighting in supposedly good causes have deliberately followed orders which resulted in massacres – for example, the United States firebombed Dresden and it massacred civilians at My Lai in 1968, ample proof that acts like those of O'Brien are possible within us all. O'Brien can call Winston insane and not be wrong, because, according to Party dogma, a person would have to be crazy if he, or she, opposed the wishes of the Party.

It should also be noted that shortly after World War II, researchers at Yale University conducted experiments in which subjects were to administer high voltage electric shocks to a man whom they thought was connected to a generator. If the subject was given a wrong answer, the man was to shock him and raise the voltage. Before the experiment, the subject had been told that the testee had a heart condition and had been given a sample of the punishment that would be meted out. In most cases, the subjects, with some urging, usually administered the electric shocks (even though the testee supposedly had lost consciousness) until told to stop. Society exerts a very great deal of pressure on us all to *conform*. (Consider, in this sense, Woody Allen's satire *Zelig*.) Conceivably, we too could someday be under the same social stresses as O'Brien; thus, it is also conceivable that we could be made to do the very same things as he. O'Brien told Winston that they had "gotten" him a long time ago. Inner Party members can be subject to the same brutal treatment as non-members. Their only "insurance" is power and orthodoxy.

Here, Orwell is feeding upon our greatest fears. He focuses on a character and tells us that we can trust him, and we trust him. Wrong. This trust turns out to be absolutely unwise. That person is actually our greatest enemy. Thus, Orwell wants us to mistrust anyone whom we might be tempted to cavalierly give power to, for it is only through our awareness of that man's potential danger to us that Orwell's vision of *1984* can be avoided.

## Big Brother/Emmanuel Goldstein

Emmanuel Goldstein and Big Brother are part and parcel of the same concept. They are the superhuman embodiment of the two extremes of Oceania politics. Big Brother is the titular head of Oceania, and Emmanuel Goldstein is the leader of the opponents of the Party, the Brotherhood. Yet both are similar – in the sense that they do *not* exist. There is no living person by those names. They both represent distortions of reality that is created within the novel. If one takes the position that "the Party is right" and that Oceania should, and will, rule the world, Big Brother becomes God, President, and friend in the great quest for ultimate victory. Conversely, Goldstein becomes the hated worm in the apple of Eden; he is Judas, Satan, and a personal enemy all rolled into one. For those who hate the Party, the roles are reversed. Like so much else in Oceania, anyone who takes either position, from a "goodthinker" like Parsons to a rebel like Winston, then that person is wrong. Clearly, both "men" are fictitious creations of the Party and serve as channels for aggression. Those who support one image or the other invariably wind up hating the other image. The end result is the same. The more fervently one hates Big Brother or Goldstein, the more one disbelieves in the existence of one and hates the counterpart. To support this view, it becomes necessary to believe more in "the cause" (Party or Brotherhood) and the possibility of the existence of the figurehead. Thus it – and he – becomes a reality. Unfortunately neither position has the slightest grain of truth in it, but *the believer* is effectively duped into submission to complete Orthodoxy or joins a Brotherhood administered by the Thought Police. The end result in either case is a victory for the Party.

The only person whom we meet who would know the truth – O'Brien – never tells us whether or not the Brotherhood really exists. When Winston asks him, O'Brien tells Winston that he will "never know the answer to that question." Thus, Orwell leaves us in the dark about the single most important fact about Oceania. While some people might argue that "if you do not know, you just don't know," others feel that that position is irrelevant. If the Brotherhood *does* exist, or if Big Brother or Emmanuel Goldstein exists, the effect upon Winston (and presumably ourselves, were we unfortunate enough to live in Oceania) would be the same. We would be denied what we call a human existence. Clearly, the Brotherhood is no better morally than the Party. If O'Brien is a member of the Brotherhood, he had no right to let Winston suffer as he did. It is doubtful that O'Brien is a member of the Brotherhood – especially when we consider his comment to Julia: "We may have to change your face." Julia bears an ugly scar on her face at the end of the novel.

As happens again and again in *1984*, one finds oneself affirming one position in one paragraph and then taking the antithetical viewpoint in the next paragraph. Ironically, in far too many ways, Big

Brother and Emmanuel Goldstein are the two most "real" characters in the novel. They are the only ones who cannot or will not be vaporized. They are locked in an endless struggle against each other and neither will ever win. O'Brien tells Winston, "You do not exist." And should O'Brien ever displease his peers or masters, he would cease to exist. Even Goldstein's statements would have to be edited and updated, if only to make sure he were betraying Oceania to whomever Oceania was currently at war, and, certainly his "correct predictions" would have to be reconciled to what Big Brother has declared. Essentially, these two characters are the frame upon which the ugly tapestry of 1984 hangs. They are the only consistent characters, and in that sense, they are the only "alive people" in Oceania. Orwell uses this ambivalence to undermine our credulity; he makes us accept the notion that these two sides of the same coin simultaneously exist and yet don't exist. Ironically, the most tangible human characters of the novel, Julia, Winston, and O'Brien become more accessible and real (even though they are fictional characters and don't exist).

In dealing with the differences between the Party and the Brotherhood, we should remember that we prefer the Brotherhood only because it opposes the Party. Yet neither the Party nor the Brotherhood has any clear politics other than the destruction of the other group. O'Brien tells Winston that he must be willing to commit the most gruesome atrocities in the name of the revolt. We know full well that the Party is every bit as brutal; they use prisoners of war for handgrenade tests and happily commit the most loathsome war crimes upon others while accusing their enemies of the very same crimes. This is the essential nature of 1984. Just as Winston is forced to face up to the truth about himself and his perceptions about Ingsoc, the reader is forced to accept a very gray truth: there are few essential differences between our world and Winston's, and the barriers between the two can fall very easily.

## A CRITICAL QUESTION

*Is the world of* 1984 *possible?*

Since its publication in 1949, Orwell's novel has consistently triggered heated debates about whether or not our society has become like Oceania, how accurate Orwell's predictions were, and which political parties' philosophies most resemble Ingsoc. The political right and the political left have both used *1984* as the basis for any number of attacks upon their counterparts. One should remember, however, that Orwell never tells us whether the Party's genesis grew out of the right *or* the left. The Party name of Ingsoc bears no more resemblance to socialism than it does to fascism. Even the old man in the bar cannot remember "whose fault" Ingsoc is. It doesn't matter. While both the right and the left have hailed this novel as exposing extreme intentions of the other political party, the fact of the matter is that Orwell was a very smart man and recognized that dictatorship is dictatorship – regardless of what political creed the government espouses. Never once in the novel do we hear mention of the Party's "uplifting the workers' struggle" or "saving individual rights from desecration by the Huns." There simply are *no politics* in Oceania. The central idea that Orwell tried to get across (and I think in this sense he failed to get people to realize or people tend to ignore) is the fact that Oceania can spring up from *any* society or government. Orwell places the capital right in the heart of the nations that most represent freedom and individual rights, the United States and Britain. From a historical context, Orwell looked at the ravages of World War II that had yet to be repaired, and he saw the great powers ready to do global battle again. The greatest pessimism expressed in *1984* is that war will be endless and that society will not recover its humanity. He perceived that the difference between Hitler and Stalin was negligible; a policeman looks like a policeman, and the differences between the East and the West *could* become non-existent.

What makes *1984* great literature is this universal applicability. Orwell depicted a personified reality. His imagination crystalizes this reality into tangibility; he succeeds in achieving the willing suspension of the readers' disbelief by giving a substantial basis of reality to his novel. Thus, while some writers, such as Norman Podhoretz in his essay "If Orwell Were Alive Today," maintain that Orwell would support or align himself politically with one political philosophy or party, I would submit that Orwell would remain substantially apart from any group, just as he did prior to his death. Orwell is a socialist at heart, and he was a zealot for democracy in spirit. *1984* is a call for individualism and independence from a government's structural control and social organization. We must vigilantly maintain checks on unbridled power. We cannot rely on the beneficence of the O'Briens of the world to keep their promises not "to take us to Room 101"; we must trust ourselves and the power of democracy ruled by concensus.

Orwell was amazingly accurate in some of his predictions. His perceptions about global political power shifts and the emergence of permanent zones of war have proven to be all too correct. He foresaw a nuclear arms buildup, grossly violent movies, and the use of helicopters in warfare. On other issues, he was partly right and partly wrong. He envisioned the deification of political leaders in the West, and he predicted that television would become the principal means of communication to mass audiences. He underestimated, however, its curbing effect upon audiences exposed to live footage of wars. Such footage has tended, increasingly, to make war less palatable. And Orwell completely miscalculated his prediction that science would stagnate and technological progress would stall.

Some of the more interesting creations in the novel include: the Two Minutes Hate, letters which can be checked off instead of written, and speakwrite (which has yet to be invented). Orwell's use of acronyms and short-form names for complex ideas and devices, however, (radar, NATO, Superfund, FBI, etc.,) show us how rapidly we have come to rely on new abbreviations for new concepts which we accept as commonplace today. But we have not sacrificed old words to replace them.

The chief concern of today's readers is directed to the feasibility of the society of Oceania itself. Can that happen here? The *technology* of Ingsoc is already here with us today. Indeed, we have surpassed it. The internal mental mechanisms of doublethink, blackwhite, and crimestop are the real glue that hold it all together. We use variations of these concepts for everyday occurrences: "I'll pretend I didn't see what I thought I saw" and "If he said it's true, then I believe him." These illustrate that we use self-control devices similar to those in *1984* to alter our perceptions or stop us from doing things we shouldn't do or think we shouldn't do. The difference is that our government does not train us to use this practice every day concerning our political opinions. Nor are these psychological devices directly used to control our *political* behavior. But they very easily could be. Human beings are extremely susceptible towards certain media, and we tend to believe whatever is said by the media. Many studies show that our political opinions are developed from "opinion leaders"—peers whose views we accept and take as our own. In our complex society, we are forced to rely on these others (in the media) for information. The risk which we run is that our best interests are not always the foremost concern of those who supply us with this information.

There are some who take the position that we already live in Oceania and that we are being controlled and ordered about by the powers that be. Others maintain the opposite position and hold that we, as individuals, control our own fate and destiny. Obviously, there is room for innumerable views between these two extremes. Nor is it implausible to use doublethink and believe in both positions concurrently. Evidence supporting both views can be found co-existing practically anywhere. We are free to stand on the street corner and criticize the government, but if we become too rabid or noisy, we will likely be arrested by the police. Some members of our society, because of dress, race, or physical characteristics, bear a presumption of being "dangerous." People in three-piece suits are seldom arrested for disturbing the peace. This dichotomy of freedom and authority is pervasive in our society. Ideally, there should be a balance for the peaceful resolution of these conflicting demands which would preserve our current system. It is our greatest strength, and if we fail to resolve conflicts peacefully, that would be our greatest vulnerability.

Orwell's vision is pessimistic, and its plausibility makes us all the more squeamish to look full-face at its possible fulfillment. We look at 1984 and see the price of negligence and unrestrained trust. Oceania, once in place, cannot be reversed. Once we make our great mistake and forget our duty to act for ourselves and watch those whom we set to watch for us, the boot will stamp down upon our faces—forever.

Oceania relies upon control of reality to maintain its control over the populace. This control is made possible by denying people of Oceania access to the truth. Thus, no one has any idea what is really going on in the world. In the middle of Hate Week (a perverted St. Valentine's Day), a speaker changes from one enemy, Eurasia, to the other, Eastasia, in mid-sentence. His actual speech never changes in substance or form; only one word is substituted for another. Yet the change is accepted by everyone within minutes. The Ingsoc maxim "He who controls the past controls the present, and he who controls the present controls the future" is shown to be devastatingly effective. As Winston writes his journal, he is not even sure whether it is 1984 or not. It is impossible for him to prove this fact, one way or another. Yet he daily aids, and sometimes he derives great pleasure, in fabricating lies. His grip on reality is as tenuous as his grip on the glass crystal. The truth has been altered beyond all recognition. As memories fade and written records are destroyed and altered, all touch with truth becomes permanently lost. The Party's truth can be foisted on the populace because there is nothing remotely cohesive or accurate enough to compete with it. Thus, it is no surprise that Julia believes that the Party invented the airplane; in a few more years, the Party can even claim that the Party has *always* existed and no one can prove them wrong. Winston and those who try to remember have no proof and, if they rebel, they are destroyed.

Adolph Hitler once boasted that if you tell a lie enough times, people will accept it as being the truth. Truth is a very delicate thing. It is subject to an individual's own perceptions and the perceptions of society at large. In the 1400s, it was not wise to profess to believe that the world was round; that view was considered to be heresy, and heretics were tortured and burned at the stake. There are many people today who do not believe that Neil Armstrong ever walked on the moon. Truth can be espoused by many sources, and each person chooses his own sources in which to believe. Orwell demonstrates the danger of having only one outside source for one's information and facts. The populace comes to rely on that one source as being right — no matter if every word of it is false. The Party will go to any lengths to enforce its version. Since there are no laws or even any objective concern as to what the Party is doing to its own people, the monopoly on truth is unchallenged, and it, in turn, evolves into a monopoly of power.

Truth is an important tool in the hands of the Party. It is the center for controlling the populace and enforcing its desire for absolute power on the people of Oceania. There can be no resistance to such a system, for the very *idea* of resistance cannot be formulated. People are forbidden to communicate or are afraid to do so; therefore, any possibility of rebellion is doomed at its inception. The Inner Party members are as badly deluded by their lies as the most stupid Outer Party members. They won't change anything. The proles know nothing and won't change anything either. Worse yet, since the only way to fight these lies is to totally disbelieve them, prospective rebels in a non-existent Brotherhood finally fall into the hands of the Thought Police.

The erosion of factual truth is an extremely dangerous quality in our society. Potentially, our values and knowledge become undermined, and we risk having a "truth" imposed upon us by an O'Brien or his Party.

## ALIENATION IN *1984*

The bewildering and anti-human existence of a person living in a totalitarian state is likely to bring about the kind of alienation that we see in *1984*. Winston, the first and most obvious example, is severely cut off from everyone else in the world. He is alone and lonely. Even with Julia, Winston does not find someone who shares the exact same feelings and thoughts that he does. Winston's wife becomes the archetype by which Winston expresses his deep and nearly psychotic hatred for women. The Party's war against love and sex has succeeded in cutting off Winston from half of the human race. He has only small recollections of his father. He has terminal guilt about starving his sister to death, and he secretly feels that he killed his mother. In this context, Winston's psychological and sexual life has been crippled. Julia is also alienated. This is clearly shown by her rebellion and her lack of friends or family.

This state of anomie (an absence of all social norms) is exactly what the Party wants. Winston is able to perform his duties for the Party without thought or question. He represses every contrary thought in the vain hope that he will not be "discovered" by the Thought Police. He is in deplorable health, and our first glimpse of him is that of a man ready to die; Winston is so ambivalent about his own existence that he would do nothing to save his own life. He muses about the how's and why's of Party control; secretly, however, he fears the truth of there being no why or wherefore; his journal is his attempt to leave some record of the evil of Ingsoc before he dies. Yet what Winston writes is little more than rambling nothings. He is unable to express his own feelings; he is, seemingly, completely alienated from himself and his own feelings. Only when he is drunk can he write such statements as: "Down with Big Brother."

Alienation is usually not an active process by which someone is walled away into a little room and left there to never come out. Rather, alienation is usually a passive process. It is a response to a world which cannot be endured. It is an unconscious stepping into that little room and shutting the door behind oneself. It is a spiritual stepping away from the rest of the world and planning to never return – or worse, like Winston, not knowing that you ever left. There is another possibility: we can be left behind by rapid change and by our inability to socially adapt. *1984* offers us the proposition that the government excludes each and every member of its society from one another. While the same has been said of our own country, I think the best example of this condition is Russia's choosing to oppress its people by economic privation, police intimidation, and surveillance. The worst criticism that can be made of our own government is its choosing not to do enough for its poor. This fundamental difference, while being tenuous, is, however, real and important. There are finite bounds on what government can and cannot do. If this sounds like a tirade against the Soviet Union, it is meant to be; there are an estimated four million people in the Gulag Archipelago prison work camps. Our own society, of course, is not without its faults, and it will probably never be perfect. But, foremost, *1984* was meant as a warning to all of us what life can be like if we cavalierly forget what civil and human rights are and what precious privileges they are. In the character of Winston Smith, Orwell shows us the destruction of the individual who cannot adjust to an insane society.

The level of alienation that pervades a society is an indication of the lack of overall wholesomeness of life in that society. A sick or depraved society will engender far more alienation than a healthy one. Orwell shows us that life in Oceania is dreary agony. The people have been reduced to a lower level of civilization; they have become little more than urban savages. The war that is supposedly being fought with East Asia or Eurasia is mirrored by the war between individuals within the Party. There are purges every two years. There are no "rocks" on which to root oneself. The glass crystal paperweight, symbolic of Winston's life as a living, loving person, is immediately smashed when Winston and Julia are arrested. Winston has no family; the Party offers itself as a surrogate, but Big Brother is little, if any, comfort. Winston's wife, mother, and sister are all out of his life. His sexual life consists of a quick foray with an occasional prostitute; he even hates his neighbors. Winston hates women and children. This is quite a large part of humanity; perhaps not surprisingly, Julia hates women also. Oceania teaches the individual to hate himself. The lonely and confused person is the ideal Party member, for he or she is intellectually and spiritually dead. This type of person is a mindless drone that can be easily led and made to do anything.

It is interesting to note the alienation of an Inner Party member like O'Brien. O'Brien, despite all of his power, has also been tortured by the Thought Police, and he must fear that his authority can be challenged and that he can be purged, like Aaronson and others. He can turn off his telescreen, but if he leaves it off too long, he will fall under suspicion. His perch is a high one within the Party, but it is every bit as shaky as Winston's. O'Brien is severely deluded by the Party's rhetoric and propaganda. Even though he has the closest view of the truth, he uses doublethink, blackwhite, and crimestop to keep himself orthodox. But he will not be able to do it forever; the retirement plan of the Party is a bullet in the back of the head. There is continual pressure from younger, more aggressive members of the Inner Party. We never know whether or not O'Brien has a wife, but Julia tells us that Inner Party members have been known to have little affairs, and we may presume that this evidences dissatisfaction and alienation with their way of life. An Inner Party member is as helpless to change things as anyone else is.

The price of alienation is severe. A totally alienated person is never able to be happy and adjusted in life. In the most severe cases, like Winston, there is a pathological death wish. In lesser instances, like Julia, alienation is a necessary retreat to harmonize the role which society makes one play and the role that one "wants" to be in. In the artificial and uncompassionate society of Oceania, there is no one and nothing to reach out to for help. It is when despair and psychosis set in that the more extreme and unhealthy symptoms of O'Brien and Winston become manifest.

Alienation is a sign of the greater sickness of the society and of the individuals within that society. It is a signpost that a society is on the road to Oceania. As our world becomes increasingly more complex and as we become increasingly less able to involve ourselves in every facet, we must be wary of our society's becoming inundated with too many barriers between its members and a population of lonely, alienated people who might be vulnerable enough to accept the promises of a Big Brother's political party.

# LOVE IN *1984*

The success or failure of love is frequently used by authors as a measure by which the success or failure of a character or characters are judged. The classic stories of literature use love in its various forms; the example which usually springs first into everyone's mind is *Romeo and Juliet*. The unsuccessful or unfulfilled love is generally considered tragic; the successful instances are usually happy or comic. The love that exists in *1984* expresses the moral and political issues central to an understanding of the intellectual conflicts in the novel.

For the purposes of the argument which follows, it is necessary for the reader to accept the relationship between Julia and Winston as "fulfilling" for both of them and to ignore any shortcomings which may be raised about their relationship. The obvious immaturity and shallowness of the portrayal of their love can be viewed as intentional or unintentional; for our purposes, let us look at Winston and Julia as people who have been emotionally crippled by their experiences and are incapable of having or expressing certain emotions and feelings.

The romance of Julia and Winston is sticky sweet; it reminds us of first kisses and carrying books home after school. In the harsh and unnourishing climate of Oceania, *emotional* love is a crime of treasonous proportions. The state wants procreational sex and nothing else: "a slightly disgusting minor operation, like having an enema." The responses of Julia and Winston to each other can be better understood if we look upon lust as a luxury item that costs a great deal, and in Oceania that price is very steep. Each taste becomes more dear to the taster. Given the fact that the Party would never allow two people who love each other to marry, the best which two people can hope for is an occasional, dangerous liaison; the downside of this situation is the possibility that one lover might denounce the other to the Thought Police.

The futility of love in a society so hostile to the needs of its people is obvious. We are assured of never being happy. The state is opposed to any feeling that it does not control. Since emotional responses are often the foundation for thought, the state hopes that by regulating all feelings, it will control all thought. The goal of the Party is power. If people are unable to be happy and the state is able to continue their misery, the state is the greatest power in peoples' lives. It is able to intrude itself into the most private parts of their lives and, thus, dominate the elemental desire and right of individuals to associate with and love whomever they like. The Party cannot allow variations of their absolute control to exist. To relinquish control of any part of the individual is to relinquish all control over the individual, and the Party will never allow that.

Remember, too, that hate and love are the opposite sides of the same coin. The state very carefully channels hatred and love in the opposite directions from where they should be going. This diversion of feelings is effected by the Anti-Sex League and the Two Minutes Hate and by Hate Week. By insuring that people who don't love each other get married to each other, the state fosters sour relations that will, at best, be an uneasy truce or, better still, will result in outright hostility and mistrust between mates. In such an atmosphere, the average person can find love and companionship only in the vile arms of the Party. Winston thinks about killing his wife. He chooses not to do this, but he is unable to live with her and thus, they separate.

Love takes many faces. There can be as many different types of love as there are relations. There is the love between a father and a son, between a brother and a sister, and between a husband and a wife. There are inanimate examples as well. One can love paintings, french fries, and a country. Orwell's treatment of love in 1984 attempts to deal with all of those feelings. Winston has numerous relationships; each is exemplary of certain kinds of love. To make Winston's tragedy complete, all of his relationships fail. Orwell frames his story upon the structure of family love. At the opposite ends of Oceania's political field are "two brothers": the Brotherhood (run by the Thought Police) and Big Brother. As the only two available public attractions, both are dangerous paths to trod. There is no mercy in the Party's dictionary. The viciousness of the Party leads to absolute loyalty or absolute rebellion and, as the examples of Parsons and Winston demonstrate, there is the final "trip to Room 101."

Family love in 1984 is an equally hollow and empty vessel of emotional expression. The degradation of poverty, caused by the Party's desire to enslave and insure power for the Inner Party, has turned the love of family into a vicious fight for food, shelter, and what little affection that can be shown. Children are no more loyal than pirates. The Party's power is maintained by fostering an anarchy of misery and unhappiness. Winston suffers tremendous guilt about starving his baby sister to death. His wife has left him for parts unknown, and he is prevented from marrying the one person whom he does love. Oddly and ironically enough, in the social sadism of Oceania, if Winston had applied to marry Julia when he hated her, their marriage would have been approved.

The control mechanisms of the Party work. After noting the foregoing, one can conclude that the Party has all of its bases covered. It is only in this light that we can appreciate how Julia and Winston's liaison gains its stature as a political act. As O'Brien tells us, the Party does not accept any unorthodox thought. This elevates Winston and Julia's lovemaking to high treason. It is sad to note that many of the instances of 1984's being censored in the United States are a direct result of this relationship – that is, critics have objected to "adultery," yet it is this very passage advocating adultery that is Orwell's target, and these unthinking critics miss this preeminent fact about the novel. Orwell's novel, above all, is a call for a *return to morality*. By portraying an immoral and evil society as a satanic act against humanity, Orwell is calling for a return to decency and morality. Winston and Julia *would* get married – if they could. Oceania is at war with every single traditional value that our culture holds dear. Orwell goes out of his way to leave us with the feeling that a person with any sort of normal, moral, and ethical value could not survive within the world of 1984. It should be a point of pride that you or I would be among the first to be hauled off to Room 101. This means that the Party is foiled from ever forming merely by our holding onto our rights and beliefs. Regardless of what they are, as long as there is more than one opinion and people are willing to support it, we will avoid the danger of totalitarianism.

Love and hatred rule the world. A true totalitarian state will attempt to intrude into these areas of our lives. We must never allow our personal feelings and relationships to be subdued by others – especially by a government. In order to prevent Ingsoc from intruding into our lives, we must prevent government from having any interference with our personal relationships. We must hold onto our freedom to love whomever we choose to. This is the *only* way we can avoid the terror of 1984.

# PLOT, STYLE, AND STRUCTURE

Orwell deliberately keeps the plot in *1984* simple. There are no narrative twists or shocking surprises until the very end when we receive the rudest and most awful shock of all. If *1984* does not seem to be a "believable story," it is because of the novel's tendency toward showing us "unreal" characters interacting under foreign circumstances. Orwell is very careful to present the idea that "people are fine"; it is "our society" and "government" that are mixed up. Julia and Winston are salt-of-the-earth individuals. They are not perfect, but they live under horrible tyranny, and they both do the best they can to survive. Orwell makes sure, however, that there is no chance for them to succeed. They enjoy a few moments of what we might call a human existence, and then they are swallowed up into the unforgiving machinery of the Party.

The plot is not merely boy-gets-girl, boy-loses-girl, and boy-and-girl go to Room 101. Plot is the narrative thread which pulls the characters through the story. A disjoined or incoherent story would never be able to effectively tell a story the way a tightly wound, well managed tale would do so.

For Orwell's purposes, the story need not be too complex, for it might distract from the parts of his *message*, about which he is more involved and concerned. By keeping the time-frame of *1984* to a short period, involving relatively few protagonists, Orwell focuses the reader's attention on the important issues of totalitarianism and control of a civilian population through brainwashing. If Orwell's story makes the reader come away with nothing more than a healthy suspicion about government and its "benevolence," the world of *1984* can be allayed.

While the plot of the novel is not complex, it is allegorical—just as Orwell uses a fable in *Animal Farm* to describe how "Big Brother" gets started, here he uses an allegorical story of an old man coming back to life through love to tell the story of what life is like after the Secret Police take over. *1984* is very much like a puzzle of Chinese boxes. Its intricacies cannot be examined and addressed without dealing with the other sides of the puzzle. The entire puzzle can be understood only as viewed as a part of the whole.

Finally, the plot of this story is not a specific function: it is meant to include "signposts" to the reader. The love story carries us past the rocky unreality of a world standing on its head. We wind up falling into the channels which are left open to Winston. We hope that there is hope with the proles, and we hope that the Brotherhood will be strong enough to overthrow Oceania. Ultimately, our hopes are, finally, crushed like Winston's for we discover that there is no hope whatsoever.

In connection with the plot of this novel, Orwell's setting is of supreme importance, for the setting of a novel creates the ambience of a story. It is Orwell's imaginary prospective that creates the depth and color which makes this novel a microcosm which pulls the reader into the writer's world. The setting can destroy or clarify points of interest. It is a tool that enables the writer to get his message across; it is extremely useful. Orwell's setting in *1984* is well done. As a master of his craft, his setting is an integral part of the fabric of his novel.

This particular setting is composed of many elements – time, place, weather, and colors being its key elements. Our response to ideas and actions are influenced by the setting. The setting helps formulate our opinions about what we are reading. *1984* starts off in spring, a time of warming rebirth and, traditionally, romance. The clock strikes *thirteen*, rather than the more traditional twelve. Thirteen has been traditionally associated with unnaturalness and bad luck; furthermore, the air is cold, we are in London, and the city is a ruin. With just those few tidbits of information, we are brought to an awareness of what this novel stands for. The city that is central to the Western tradition has been, and is still being, destroyed. Everything – from the language and culture to its history and people – is being raped and demolished. With the first sentence of the novel, Orwell tells us that the world has been turned upon its head, and we are about to go on a voyage into a cold and loveless place, where we will meet a lonely man named Winston Smith.

We are instantly aware of the topsy-turvy world because of the setting. Our interaction takes place at a conscious and unconscious level. Even if you are not reading for detail, the idea of an anti-human world comes across through the events and the words of the characters. We know the Ministry of Love is a place of darkness long before the notion occurs to Winston. Orwell uses setting to communicate mood and situations. The Golden Country is light and colorful; it is so vastly different from the drab and ugly London that we feel the elation of Winston and Julia's mutually awakening feelings of love. This birth of new life could take place only away from the London of *1984*.

Orwell uses setting to make our natural feelings hate Ingsoc and Big Brother. Orwell describes things in clinical, straightforward ways and then infuses us into a world of unrelenting fury. The best examples of this are the Two Minutes Hate and Winston's electroshock treatment. Orwell's characters are arrayed in the relaxing setting of people watching a film or a man lying on a stretcher. We expect people to watch a movie; we don't expect them to go berserk and scream. We expect Winston to be cared for; instead, he is brutally tortured. Orwell tells us that the movie is about the bombing of a lifeboat. The Party members actually cheer! By giving us normal surroundings and then by twisting them savagely, Orwell communicates the idea that our own world is vulnerable and others might seek to do to our world what the Party has done to Oceania.

Orwell takes particular delight in rubbing our noses in the dirt and filth of Oceania. He describes apartment complexes as having ghastly stenches. London may be one of the most beautiful cities in the world, but in *1984*, it is an open sewer. Rats and vermin are there to remind us that things which we value, things such as freedom and health, are intentionally absent in Oceania; there are only things we don't like: rats, bugs, pestilence, filth, and oppression.

This novel's setting, then, affects the way that we feel about ideas and people. In *1984*, Orwell manipulates his setting to influence the reader to hate the Party. When this hate is translated into reality, after the reader has lain the book down, the reader carries Orwell's ideas and feelings about totalitarianism into life; hopefully, the reader will instinctively react against any mechanism or idea that smacks of Oceania. Or, at the very least, the reader will carry a defensive cynicism, and he will warily approach anything which resembles totalitarianism.

Orwell's style is a counterpart to his enormous imagination. He writes like a lumberjack; his words are his ax, which slices through the air and slams onto his target with a resounding "thud." His words and the style which he uses are powerful and overwhelming. He describes pain and suffering in graphic detail; we feel each punch, kick, and shock. Winston's torture is very real and tangible to the reader. While Orwell can be indirect or symbolic in presenting some concepts, his presentation keeps the reader alert by shifting suddenly to exciting or unexpected directions. The most chilling example of this is the echo of Winston's words in the room over Charrington's shop: "You are the dead."

Orwell's language is extremely violent. Death, pain, maiming, killing, and butchery pervade every paragraph. He knows his subject perfectly, and while it seems that he sometimes rams his ideas down the reader's throat, he has a bitter message to pass on, and he doesn't want to sugarcoat it. He is not the least bit sorry; he wants his readers to become enraged, furious, and ready to rip down any vestige of Ingsoc that presents itself. Such intentions do not allow pretty pictures; the world of *1984* is a dirty world, and Orwell literally seizes the murk right off the page and thrusts it into the reader's psyche.

Great writers are magicians who entrance their readers. Orwell is extremely compelling. He pulls at his reader's heartstrings. He falsely raises a hope and then smashes it down before our eyes. He weaves us in between war crimes and sweet idylls. *1984* is a voyage between the reality of our world, the unreality of fiction, and the full range of possibilities in between. Orwell is seeking discovery and satisfaction. He seeks to drive a stake through the heart of the vampire of tyranny. The barrier between what is real to him and what he wants to depict in his novel fades and allows Orwell to satirize and mimic contemporary society and send out his message to the world.

*1984* expresses a full range of human emotions. There is humor and tears, and there is also shock and bitterness. We *feel* as we read. In this sense, the novel takes on a life beyond the borders of a paperback novel with off-white pages and black print. There is real interaction between the book, the reader, and the ideas and feelings that develop.

Orwell's style is the spell which takes us into the "reality" of the world of *1984*. It cannot be discounted as just a few good ideas and words which have come to describe our own times. Doublethink, Big Brother, and other phenomenons within *1984* have all come to be key descriptions of our own times. The success of this novel can be measured by its extensive publication, its extensive repression, and the frequency that it is raised in issues relating to freedom. If success were to be measured in impact alone, *1984* is a smash hit. Orwell has written a novel which has achieved a life of its own—apart from its being a novel. People who have never read the novel are aware of the novel and many of the concepts which it presents. It should also be noted that *1984* is used by every part of the political spectrum: its universality and flexibility allow this novel to be applied to almost anything. Orwell's style is important to note, for anyone writing something that is supposed to have a strong impact should remember Orwell's style as a model to follow.

If style and symbolism are the color and patina to a novel, then structure is, just like it sounds, the pillars, girders, beams, and foundations of the novel. Structural analysis of a novel attempts to describe the novel based upon the author's central themes and ideas. In a complex work such as *1984*, there are numerous structural relationships present. Orwell delves into politics, economics, war, love, friendship, and truth, to name a few of his subjects. His investigations are rooted into the very fiber of the novel. In the microcosm of *1984*, the love between Winston and Julia is exemplary of a society without love and the struggle of those who have to exist within that society and who try to find fulfillment under harsh conditions. Orwell builds and interlocks his ideas into a coherent story. He creates the concepts of Ingsoc, and he rationally demonstrates that madness *can* be power. The apparatus of the Party is designed to set into play the conflict between truth and the mutability of the past. The alienation of our normative values is also a natural result of this device. Each intellectual block is stacked and glued together for support. Orwell's dystopia has height, width, and breadth; it is a three-dimensional parody of what our society *can* become. Its basis on reality is strong enough to hammer home the idea that totalitarian government is *real* and that our society can all too easily be subverted into such a monstrosity.

*1984* has many purposes, and its structure allows it to do them all at once. It is an educational story; it deals with the entire spectrum of twentieth-century politics; it makes a statement about the enduring qualities of love, and all of this is done through narrative fiction, decorated in horrific detail. The importance of the message, coupled with the artistry of its execution has made it an enduring and controversial tour de force. Orwell's hatred for hypocrisy and for social lies has spawned a novel which has been used to smear all ends of the modern political spectrum. There are aspects of "the Party" in every decision made for a power play. Since every political entity makes certain decisions, by fiat, which attempt to influence our lives, elements of the Party can be ascribed to them all. This has the destructive tendency of fostering mistrust of *all* political proceedings. But the novel has a constructive side as well, for high-handed politics are inherently despised for their resemblance to *1984*.

The best evidence of the structural integrity of *1984* is witnessed by the fact that the novel can be analyzed in its various forms and still withstand a credible discussion, regardless of the topic. There are enough meaty ideas within this novel to withstand the most probing examination. One can approach *1984* in different ways and still find more to contemplate. As our times change, and as events happen, we will be able to hold this novel up as a standard to judge other so-called enlightening "political novels." Measured against *1984*, their "lights" and promises look less bright. Within Orwell's "light" of *1984*, the clear light of truth will perhaps never look so good.

## HUMANITY AND SOCIETY IN *1984*

To demonstrate the effectiveness of Newspeak, this is a short essay on *1984*. Then it is translated into Newspeak. This demonstrates the powerful ability of Ingsoc to eliminate thought; the entire gist of the original essay is destroyed. The student of *1984* should find this to be both amusing and frightening.

George Orwell's *1984* is a bitter attack against the evil modern plague of totalitarian oppression. Orwell expresses the idea that a government may enslave its people through controlling the media and enforcing its control through an extensive police network. His protagonist is an English middle-class thinker named Winston Smith. Winston is fascinated by the intellectual process of slavery. He works in the ministry which produces most of the lies for popular consumption; this ministry is ironically called Minitrue (a short form of Ministry of Truth). Winston rebels against his masters because he is aware of the evil of the system, and he is aware of the mass deception being perpetrated by the state. Winston starts off as a lonely man writing away in his illegal journal. He tries to tell us what his world is like. Orwell describes the tremendous ugliness of his world. Winston lives in a slum and can barely afford to live. His health is poor, and one gets the feeling that he wishes that he were dead. Orwell takes Winston on a rollercoaster ride of hope and disaster. Orwell raises our hopes by having Winston fall in love, and then he systematically crushes his rebellion and leaves him as less than a human being. This essay will deal with humanity and society and what happens when humanity and society are taken away from us.

Humanity is the quality of being a human being. This implies the normal range of emotions and thoughts as well as the process of living as a human being is *presumed* to live. Society is the aggregate whole of a larger group of people. Society is the means by which people organize themselves so that they may function and live efficiently. The world of *1984* is divided into three "super states"; these states are permanently at war with each other. Winston lives in Oceania, which comprises most of what is now the United States and Great Britain. Winston lives a life of squalor; he is very lonely and his love life extends only to an occasional prostitute. The society of Oceania is split into three castes: a small group of brutal rulers, a larger group of middle-level functionaries, and a vast majority of mindless slaves; these are called respectively, the Inner Party, the Outer Party, and the Proles. The three groups are segregated, and status is based upon power. The Inner Party maintains its position through a police force which is bound by no laws. In Oceania, everything can be a crime. All opposition is punishable by death. Most societies have a set of rules that determine how we should behave; Oceania has only implied rules that may or may not be enforced on any given occasion. This situation affects Winston's humanity. Winston, who tries to maintain values similar to our own, is deprived of his humanity. He is dying of disease and malnutrition. To attempt to regain his lost humanity, he rebels; he begins writing his diary and tries to contact the mystical Brotherhood so that he might join a different society. The Brotherhood is led by the nonexistent Emmanuel Goldstein, just as the Party of Oceania is led by Big Brother. The entire society, however, is structured around lies. Winston has the very important job of altering the past and covering up the lies of the Party. Oceania will not even tell the truth about when or whom they have been at war with in the past. Thus the Party claims: we are at war with Eastasia. In truth, they have been at war with Eurasia, and Eastasia is their ally.

Winston's rebellion is discovered at its inception, and he is watched by the police until they decide to destroy him. The man whom Winston believed was his ally and friend was actually his greatest enemy. In the society of lies, he had fallen for a lie, and his punishment was his total destruction. O'Brien, Winston's betrayer, takes personal charge of Winston's destruction. One of the most important aspects of our humanity is the need for companionship and love. Winston tries to maintain his loyalty to his lover and co-conspirator; in essence, he fights for his humanity. He loses, and he is turned into something less than human.

Orwell takes the thesis that society can destroy our humanity, and in a sick, warped society, this becomes the raison d'être of the state. By the end of 1984, Winston is pointed in front of a mirror and shown the ravages of his destruction. He is told that he is dead as a man. This last message demonstrates that his status is as a non-human being, one who is only physically alive. The objective of Oceania is a homogeneous society of dead creatures who will obediently serve without question or thought.

1984 is a depressing story, but its impact is tremendous. It is a warning to us to preserve our humanity and to make sure that we live in a sane society. We must not let happen to us what happens to Winston Smith.

*This is the same essay translated into Newspeak. In order to be truly proper Newspeak, the entire aspect of the essay has to be altered to be "goodthink."*

George Orwell's 1984 is thinkcrime. Orwell duckspeak crimethink Ingsoc. Protagonist doubleplusungood oldthinker Winston Smith. Winston loves Big Brother. Winston works for Minitrue. Winston did thinkcrime. Winston did plusthinkcrimewise. Winston goodsexed. Orwell described Ingsoc doubleplusgood. Winston lived good in Oceania. Crimestop. Orwell misreport Winston goodthinker and goodsexer. Winston thinkcriminal then would be goodthinker. This essay says Ingsoc doubleplusgood.

Mans is Ingsoc. This implies goodthinking. Ingsoc is mans and process of goodthink. World of 1984 is Oceania. Winston lives in Oceania. Winston lives Ingsoc. Ingsoc is Party and proles. Ingsoc is goodthinkful Inner Party and goodthinkful Outer Party and proles. Party is Party. Proles are proles. Inner Party rules Ingsoc; thinkpol doubleplushelpwise. Thinkcrime. Brotherhood doubleplusungood opposes Party. Oceania has Ingsoc. Winston is thinkcriminal. Winston is oldthinker. Winston healthful. Oldthinker Winston does thinkcrime, joins Brotherhood. Brotherhood is Goldstein. Ingsoc structured by

Ingsoc. Winston proofread news prevent malreport. Oceania has always been at war with Eastasia. Eurasia doubleplusgood ally.

Thinkpol save Winston from thoughtcrime. Worst enemy of Winston is thinkpol friend of Winston. Good Ingsoc Winston saved ungoodness. O'Brien, Winston's savior, takes personal charge of Winston's salvation. Individual needs Ingsoc. Winston tried sexcrime with thinkcriminal. Party gives Winston mercy. Winston wins, becomes goodthinker.

Orwell shows thoughtcrime destroys Ingsoc. Ingsoc victory goodthink. Winston looked in mirror and saw penalty of thoughtcrime. Told thinkcrime doubleplusungood. Winston goodthinker. Oceania objective is Ingsoc.

*1984* is thinkcrime. It is duckspeak. Warning to preserve Oceania. We will liquidate thinkcrime.

## KEY QUOTATIONS IN *1984*

The following quotations are included because they will help you think (and re-think) about *1984*. They will enable you to see how closely you have read the novel and how well you understand it. These passages sum up major concepts and can lead to discussions about the intricacies of the novel. They can be used as practice for examinations because they represent the kind of quotes that teachers often use on tests. Think about what Orwell or the characters is trying to say and how the passage works as a means of communicating an idea or concept. The passages have been selected for artistic merit and shock value; the page numbers in parentheses refer to the Signet Classic edition of *1984*, copyright 1981, by New American Library.

"I hate purity, I hate goodness. I don't want any virtue to exist anywhere. I want everyone to be corrupt to the bones." (104)

"I knew that you were against *them*." (102)

"If you kept the small rules, you could break the big ones." (107)

"We are the dead." (113)

"Rats! In this room!" (119)

"It's a little chunk of history that they've forgotten to alter. It's a message from a hundred years ago, if one knew how to read it." (121)

"It had a savage, barking rhythm that could not exactly be called music." (123)

"Processions, meetings, military parades, lectures, waxwork displays, film shows, telescreen programs all had to be organized; stands had to be erected, effigies built, slogans coined, songs written, rumors circulated, photographs faked." (122)

"The proles . . . were being lashed into one of their periodic frenzies of patriotism." (124)

"The Party had invented airplanes." (127)

"Give your sister back her chocolate!" (135)

"If they could make me stop loving you—that would be the real betrayal." (137)

"Do it to Julia!" (236)

"To our Leader: To Emmanuel Goldstein." (141)

TWO AND TWO MAKE FIVE. (228)

"Nothing altered in his voice or manner, or in the content of what he was saying, but suddenly the names were different. . . . Oceania was at war with Eastasia!" (149)

"The two aims of the Party are to conquer the whole surface of the earth and to extinguish once and for all the possibility of independent thought." (159)

"I tried to do my best for the Party, didn't I?" (192)

# *1984* GAME PAGE AND ESSAY TOPICS

Here are some questions for you to try and answer; while there is no single right or wrong answer, these questions will help you to see how well you are able to use the ideas of the novel and apply them to the real world.

1. Take the current president of the United States and prove, first, that he is Big Brother. Now use "doublethink" and prove that he isn't.

2. Think of instances in which our thinking is controlled. Are there groups and organizations that actively use mind control? How are they similar or different from "the Party"? If you were to assume that the Party is a singularly evil entity, would you say that this group is equally evil?

3. Prove that anything is true.

4. Are we already living, in part, in the world of *1984*? If you think that we are not, why can the government exert the influence that it does? If you think that we are, why is the government allowing *1984* to still be published and read?

5. If you were George Orwell, would you be pleased or displeased with the world political scene?

6. How would you protect yourself against the Thought Police? Is there any defense? What can you do, personally, to prevent Ingsoc from becoming reality?

7. Is there any way to overthrow the Party? What would you do to stop their control? Would it work, or would it be futile?

8. You are a budding O'Brien type of person; what important career decisions would you make? What would you do with a friend like Winston?

9. Write your own essay in Newspeak. Note the differences in what you want to say and how it actually comes out. Does Newspeak

destroy thought? Does it enable the government to control people? What types of Newspeak do we use today? Does it perform the same function? Does it affect the way we do things in society?

## SELECTED BIBLIOGRAPHY

BAKKER, J. "Socialism, Art, and George Orwell," *Dutch Quarterly Review of Anglo American Letters*, Vol. 6, pp. 44-56, 1974.

BARR, ALAN. "The Paradise Behind *1984*," *English Miscellany*, Vol. 19, pp. 197-203, 1968.

BEADLE, GORDON B. "George Orwell and the Death of God," *Colorado Quarterly*, Vol. 23, pp. 51-63, 1972.

BEAUCHAMP, GORMAN. "Of Man's Last Disobedience: Zamiatin's *We* and Orwell's *1984*," *Comparative Literature Studies*, Vol. 10, pp. 285-301, 1971.

_____. "Future Words: Language and the Dystopian Novel," *Style*, Vol. 8, pp. 462-76, 1974.

BROWN, EDWARD JAMES. *Brave New World, 1984, and We.* Ann Arbor: Ardis, 1976.

CHURCH, MARGARET AND WILLIAM T. STAFFORD, eds. George Orwell Number (special issue), *Modern Fiction Studies*, Vol. 21, 1975.

CONNERS, JAMES. "Zamiatin's *We* and the Genesis of *1984*," *Modern Fiction Studies*, Vol. 21, pp. 107-24, 1975.

CRICK, BERNARD. *George Orwell: A Life.* Boston: Little, Brown, 1980.

FOWLER, ROGER, BOB HODGE, GUNTHER KRESS, AND TONY TREW. *Language and Control.* London: Routledge, 1979.

GROSS, MARIAM, ed. *The World of George Orwell.* New York: Simon and Schuster, London Wiedenfield, and Nicholson, 1972.

HOLLIS, CHRISTOPHER. *A Study of George Orwell: The Man and His Works.* Chicago: Henry Regenry, 1956.

HOWE, IRVING. "Orwell: History as a Nightmare," (in his *Politics and the Novel*). New York: Horizon, 1956.

HYNES, SAMUEL, ed. *Twentieth Century Interpretations of 1984: A Collection of Critical Essays.* Englewood Cliffs, New Jersey: Prentice-Hall, 1971.

INGLE, STEPHAN J. "The Politics of George Orwell: A Reappraisal," *Queen's Quarterly*, Vol. 80, pp. 22-33, 1972.

LEIF, RUTH A. *Homage to Oceania: The Prophetic Vision of George Orwell.* Columbus: Ohio State University Press, 1969.

ORWELL, GEORGE. *The Collected Essays and Journalism and Letters of George Orwell.* New York: Harcourt, Brace, and World, 1968.

PHILMUS, ROBERT M. "The Language of Utopia," *Studies in Literary Imagination*, Vol. 6, pp. 61-78, 1972.

PODHORETZ, NORMAN. "If Orwell Were Alive Today," *Harpers*, Vol. 267, No. 1592, 1983.

REES, RICHARD. *George Orwell: Fugitive from the Camp of Victory.* London: Secker and Warburg, 1961.

ROAZEN, PAUL. "Orwell, Freud, and *1984*," *Virginia Quarterly Review*, Vol. 54, pp. 675-95, 1976.

SANDISON, ALAN. *The Last Man in Europe: An Essay on George Orwell.* New York: Barnes and Noble, 1973.

SCRUGGS, CHARLES. "George Orwell and Jonathan Swift: A Literary Relationship," *South Atlantic Quarterly*, Vol. 76, pp. 177-89, 1976.

SMALL, CHRISTOPHER. *The Road to Miniluv: George Orwell, the State, and God.* London: Gollancz Press, 1974.

55

SMITH, MARCUS. "The Wall of Blackness: A Psychological Approach to *1984, Modern Fiction Studies*, Vol. 14, pp. 423-33, 1968.

STANSKY, PETER and WILLIAM ABRAHAMS. *The Unknown Orwell.* New York: Knopf, 1972.

SPERBER, MURRAY. "Gazing into the Glass Paperweight: The Structure and Psychology of Orwell's *1984, Modern Fiction Studies*, Vol. 26, pp. 213-26, 1980.

STEINHOFF, WILLIAM. *George Orwell and the Origins of 1984.* Ann Arbor: University of Michigan Press, 1974.

TAMBLING, VICTOR, R. S. "Following in the Footsteps of Jack London: George Orwell, Writer and Critic," *Jack London Newsletter*, 1978.

THOMAS, EDWARD M. *Orwell.* London and Edinburgh: Oliver and Boyd, 1965.

VOORHEES, RICHARD J. *The Paradox of George Orwell.* West Lafayette, Ind.: Purdue University Studies, 1961.

WILDING, MICHAEL. "Orwell's *1984*: Rewriting the Future," *Sydney Studies in English*, Vol. 2, pp. 38-63, 1976.

WILLIAMS, RAYMOND. *George Orwell.* New York: Viking, 1971.

WILLIAMS, GEORGE. *The Crystal Spirit: A Study of George Orwell.* Boston and Toronto: Little, Brown, 1966.

ZWERDLING, ALEX. *Orwell and the New Left.* New Haven and London: Yale University Press, 1974.